PIANO • VOCAL • GUITAR

CONTEMPORARY WEDDING BALLADS

ISBN 978-1-4234-8862-0

7777 W. BLUEMOUND RD. P.O. BOX 13819 MILWAUKEE, WI 53213

Visit Hal Leonard Online at
www.halleonard.com

CONTEMPORARY WEDDING BALLADS

BEAUTIFUL IN MY EYES

Words and Music by
JOSHUA KADISON

E♭/B♭
6fr
B♭
You're my
We'll have our
we can
A♭maj7
B♭/A♭
Mo - na Li - sa, you're my rain - bow skies, and my
fill of tears, our share of sighs. My
laugh a - bout how time real - ly flies. We won't
Gm7
Cm7
3fr
on - ly prayer is that you re - al - ize
on - ly prayer is that you re - al - ize
say good - bye 'cause true love nev - er dies;
Fm7
E♭/G
3fr
A♭(add9)
4fr
B♭sus
B♭
you'll al - ways be beau - ti - ful in my

1
2, 3
E♭
E♭/B♭
B♭
3fr
6fr
eyes.
eyes. You will al - ways
be beau - ti - ful in my eyes.
A♭/E♭
And the pass - ing years will show that you will al - ways
A♭
E♭/G
4fr
Fm7
grow ev - er more beau - ti - ful in my
To Coda

Eb
Fm7
Eb/G
Absus2
Bb
D.S. al Coda
(take 2nd ending)
eyes.
When there are
CODA
Eb
Bb
eyes. The pass - ing years will show that you will al - ways
Ab
Eb/G
Fm7
Bb
Eb
Fm7
grow ev - er more beau - ti - ful in my eyes.
Eb/G
Absus2
Bb
Eb
rit.

ENDLESS LOVE

Words and Music by
LIONEL RICHIE

Eb/F Fsus F Bb F/A
you're ev - 'ry step I make. And
I can't re - sist your charms. And
Ebmaj7 Eb/F F Bb F/A
3fr
3
I, I want to share all my
love, I'll be a fool for
mf
Gm Dm/F Eb Eb/F F
3fr
3fr
love with you; no one else
you, I'm sure; you know I don't
Bb Bb9 Ebmaj7
3fr
will do.
And your eyes,
mind.
'Cause you,

E♭/F
F
B♭
F/A
Gm
F6
they tell me how much you care. Oh,
you mean the world to me. Oh,
E♭
Dm7
Cm7
yes, you will al - ways be
I know I've found in you
E♭/F
1
B♭
my end - less love.
my end - less
8va
mp
2
B♭
love.
mp

E♭
3fr
E♭/F
Fsus
F
3
3
B♭
3
3
E♭
3fr
E♭/F
B♭
E♭
3fr
Oh, and love,
cresc.
mf

E♭/F
F
B♭
F/A
Gm7
F/A
I'll be that fool for you, I'm
E♭
3fr
E♭/F
F
B♭
sure; you know I don't mind.
B♭9
E♭
3fr
E♭/F
F
And yes, you'll be the
B♭
F/A
Gm
3fr
Dm/F
E♭maj7
3fr
on - ly one. No one can de - ny

Dm7
E♭maj7
3fr
Dm7
this love
I have in - side.
I'll
E♭maj7
3fr
Dm7
Cm7
3fr
give
it all to you,
my love,
my love,
E♭/F
B♭
3
my
end - less
love.
3
p
3
3
E♭
3fr
E♭/F
Fsus
F
E♭/B♭
6fr
B♭
rit.

(Everything I Do)

I DO IT FOR YOU

from the Motion Picture ROBIN HOOD: PRINCE OF THIEVES

Words and Music by BRYAN ADAMS,
R.J. LANGE and MICHAEL KAMEN

F
C/G
G
Dm
C
G♭
D♭/A♭
A♭
E♭m
D♭
find me there you'll _ search _ no more. Don't tell me it's not worth fight-ing
give it all, I would sac - ri - fice. Don't tell me it's not worth fight-ing
Dm
C/D
Dm
C
E♭m
D♭/E♭
E♭m
D♭
for. You can't tell me, it's not worth dy - ing
for. I can't help it, there's noth - ing I want
C
D♭
for.
more.
You know it's true, ev - 'ry - thing I
Gsus
3fr
A♭sus
1 C5
3fr
D♭5
do, I do it for _ you.

2
C
Csus
C
B♭
D♭
D♭sus
D♭
C♭
you.
There's
no
love
like
E♭
B♭
F♭
C♭
your
love,
and
no
oth
-
er
could
give
F
C
G♭
D♭
more
love.
There's
no
way,
un
-
less
G
D
A♭
E♭
you're
there
all
the
time,
all
the

G
Gsus
F(add2)
A♭
A♭sus
G♭(add2)
way, yeah.
C
D♭
F(add2)
G♭(add2)
C
D♭
Dm
G
Gsus
G
E♭m
A♭
A♭sus
A♭
Oh, you can't tell me it's not worth try - ing for. I can't

Dm G C Csus C
E♭m A♭ D♭ D♭sus D♭
help it, there's noth-ing I want more. Yeah, I would fight for you, I'd
G Gsus G F
A♭ A♭sus A♭ G♭
lie for you, walk the mile for you, yeah, I'd
Fm C/G
G♭m D♭/A♭
die for you. You know it's true, ev - 'ry - thing I
Gsus G F F6 C
A♭sus A♭ G♭ G♭6 D♭
do, oh, oh, I do it for you.
rit.

BLESS THE BROKEN ROAD

Words and Music by MARCUS HUMMON,
BOBBY BOYD and JEFF HANNA

Am7
G
F
C/E
Dm7
G7sus
I got lost a time or two, wiped my brow and kept push-in' through.
C/E
Fsus2
G
Am
F
F/G
C
I could-n't see how ev-er-y sign point-ed straight to you.
Dm
C/E
F6
C/F
3fr
C
Dm
C/E
G
G7
C
But ev-er-y long lost dream led me to where you are.
Dm
C/E
F
C/F
3fr
Am7
G/B
C
Dm7
C
Oth-ers who broke my heart, they were like north-ern stars

G C Dm C/E F C/F 3fr C Dm C/E G G7 Am
pointing me on my way into your loving arms.
G/B C Dm7 C/E Fsus2 C/F 3fr
This much I know is true: that
To Coda
C/E F G Am F F/G C/E Fsus2
God blessed the broken road that led me straight to you.
G Am F F/G C/G C C/E Fsus2
Yes, He did.

G
Am7
F
F/G
C/G
C
C/E
Fsus2
I think a - bout the years
G
Am
F
G
C
C/E
Fsus2
I've spent just pass- in' through.
I'd like to have the time
G
Am
F
F/G
C
Am11
3fr
I lost and give it back to you.
But you just smile and take
G
F
C/E
Dm7
F/G
C/E
Fsus2
my hand. You've been there, you un - der - stand it's all part of a grand -

D.S. al Coda
G
Am
F
F/G
C
Dm
C/E
- er plan
that is
com - in'
true.
Ev - er - y
CODA
N.C.
F/C
C
F(add9)
C
G
C
F
Am
Dm
C
G/B
C
F
F(add9)
C
Now I'm just a - roll - in' home

G
Am
G/B
C
into my lover's arms.
This much I
Dm7
C/E
Fsus2
C/F
3fr
C/E
Fsus2
know is true:
that God blessed the bro-
G
Am
F
F/G
C/E
Fsus2
-ken road that led me straight to you,
G
Am
F
F/G
C/G
C
C/E
Fsus2
that God blessed the bro-

G
Am
F
G
- ken road
that led me straight
3
3
C/E
Fsus2
G
Am
to you.
F
F/G
C/G
C
C/E
Fsus2
G
Am
F
F/G
C
rit.

FROM THIS MOMENT ON

Words and Music by SHANIA TWAIN
and R.J. LANGE

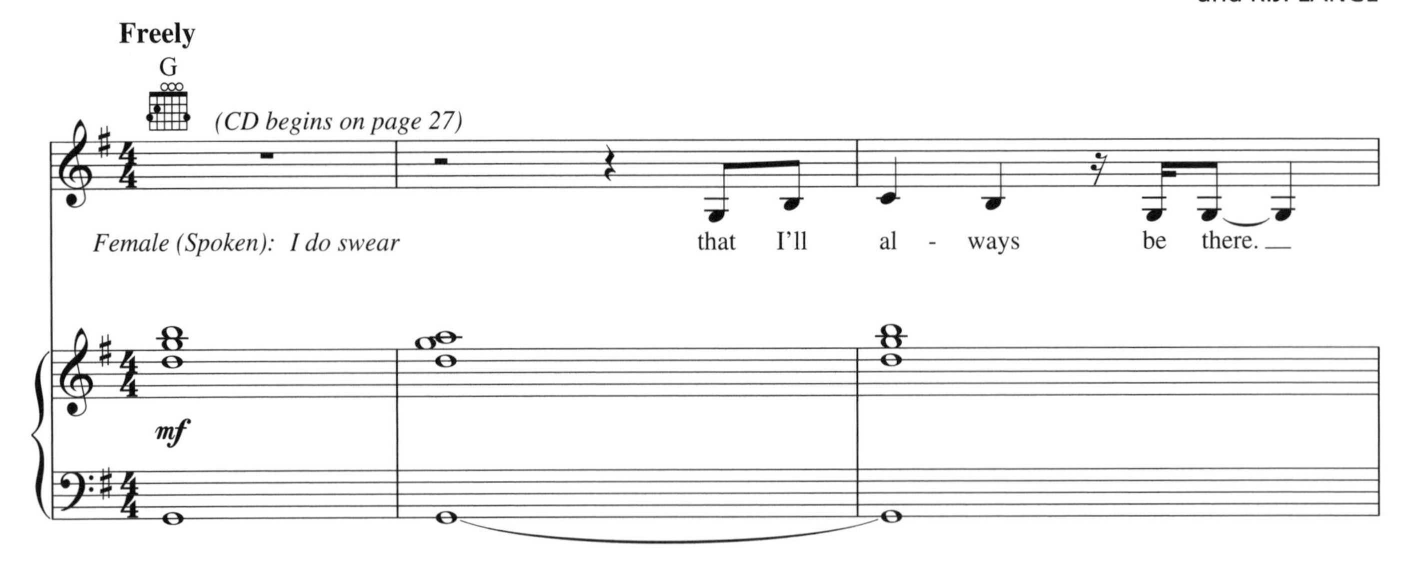
Freely
G
(CD begins on page 27)
Female (Spoken): I do swear
that I'll al - ways be there.
mf

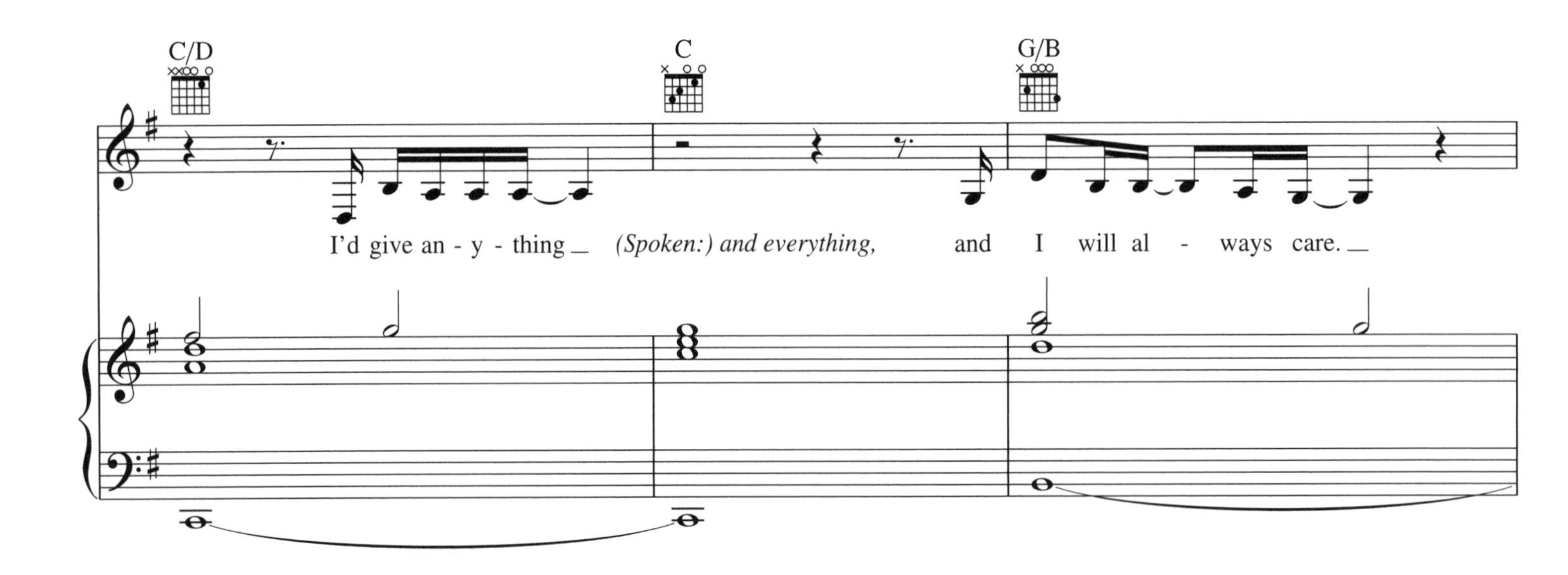
C/D
C
G/B
I'd give an - y - thing
(Spoken:) and everything,
and I will al - ways care.

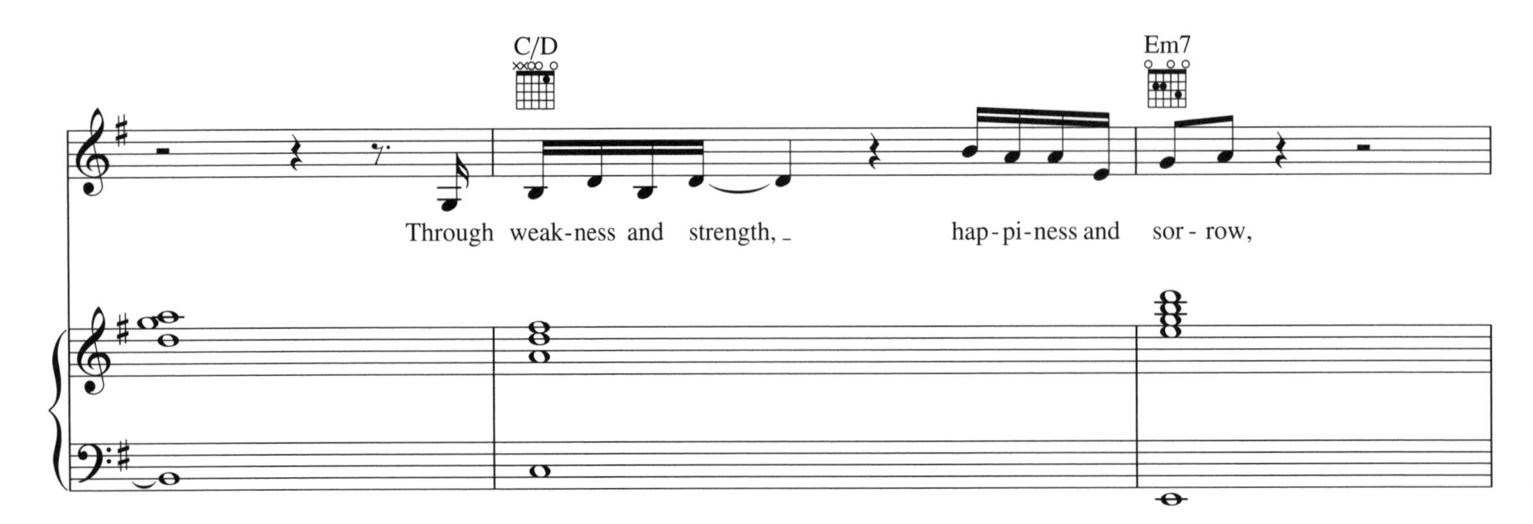
C/D
Em7
Through weak-ness and strength,
hap-pi-ness and sor - row,

D/F♯
D/G
G
(Spoken:) for better, for worse, I will love you
with ev - 'ry beat of my heart.
C
D
G/C
(CD begins here)
N.C.
From this
Slowly
G5
3fr
C(add2)
mo - ment
life has be - gun.
*Male:
From this mo - ment
D5
5fr
C(add2)
G5
3fr
you are the one.
Female:
Right be - side you
Both:
is where I be - long,
*Male vocals sung an octave higher throughout.

Am
D
G5
3fr
from this mo - ment on.
Male: From this mo - ment I have been blessed.
C(add2)
D5
5fr
Female:
I live on - ly for your hap - pi - ness.
Male:
And for your
C(add2)
G5
3fr
Am
D
Both:
love I'd give my last breath,
from this mo - ment on.
C(add2)
G
C(add2)
Female: I give my hand to you with all my heart.
Male: Can't

D/F#
G
wait to live my life with you, can't wait to start.
C(add2)
Em7
Both:
You and I will nev - er be a - part.
My dreams came true
C(add2)
G
G/D
D
N.C.
be - cause of you.
Female:
From this
A(add2)
E
D
mo - ment, Both: as long as I live, I will love you, I

E
D
A
promise you this. There is nothing I wouldn't give,
Bm
E
D(add2)
D/E
A
F♯m7
from this moment on.
D(add2)
E
A
Female: You're the reason I believe in
D
E
love, Male: and you're the answer to my prayers from

A
up a - bove.
Both: All we need is just the two of
D
F♯m7
D(add2)
us. My dreams came true be - cause
A
A/E
E
N.C.
of you. From this
B
F♯
mo - ment, as long as I live, I will

E
F♯
E
love you, I promise you this. There is nothing I wouldn't give,
B
C♯m
4fr
F♯
E(add2)
from this moment. Female: I will love you, Male: I will love you Female: as
B
C♯m
4fr
F♯
long as I live, Both: from this mo - ment
E(add2)
B/D♯
4fr
F♯7
B
Female: on.
Male: on.
Female: Mm, Both: mm.
rit.

HAVE I TOLD YOU LATELY

Words and Music by
VAN MORRISON

Cm7
3fr
B♭
E♭/F
ease my trou-bles, that's what you do.
For the
Instrumental solo
B♭
Dm7
E♭
3fr
E♭/F
morn - in' sun in all its glo - ry greets the
B♭
Dm7
E♭
3fr
E♭/F
day with hope and com-fort, too.
E♭maj7
3fr
Dm7
You fill my life with laugh - ter and some-how you make it bet - ter,

Cm7
E♭/F
B♭
Cm7
B♭/D
3fr
ease my trou - bles, that's ___ what you do.
Solo ends
E♭maj7
There's a love that's di - vine
and it's yours and it's mine ___
Dm7
Cm7
Dm7
E♭maj7
___ like the sun.
And at the end of the day
Dm7
1
E♭/F
we should give thanks and pray ___ to the one, _
to the one. _
Have I
3

2
E♭/F
B♭
Dm7
to the one. And have I told you late - ly that I
E♭
E♭/F
B♭
Dm7
love you? Have I told you there's no one else a -
E♭
E♭/F
E♭maj7
bove you? You fill my heart with glad - ness,
Dm7
Cm7
E♭/F
take a - way my sad - ness, ease my trou - bles, that's what you
3fr

Bb
Cm7
Bb/D
Ebmaj7
do. Take a - way all my sad - ness,
Dm7
Cm7
Bb
Cm7
Bb/D
fill my life with glad - ness, ease my trou-bles, that's what you do.
Ebmaj7
Dm7
Take a - way all my sad - ness, fill my life with glad - ness,
Cm7
Eb/F
Bb
ease my trou - bles, that's what you do.
rall.

HERE AND NOW

Words and Music by TERRY STEELE
and DAVID ELLIOT

G(add9)/B
B7/D♯
Em7
G/B
Cmaj9
Hold - ing you close through the night, I need you.
C/D
G(add9)
Yeah.
I look in your
I look in your
F♯m7♭5
4fr
B7♭9
Em7
D
eyes, and there I see what
eyes, there I see
C(add9)
C/D
G(add9)
hap - pi - ness real - ly means. The love that we
all that a love should real - ly be. And I need you

F#m7b5
B7b9
Cmaj7
G/B
share makes life so sweet. To -
more and more each day.
C(add9)/E
Cm6/Eb
G/D
C(add9)
geth - er we'll al - ways be.
Noth - ing can take your love a - way.
G(add9)/B
B7/D#
Em7
G/B
This pledge of love feels so right, and, ooh, I need
More than I dare to dream. I need
Cmaj9
F#m7b5
A/B
Cmaj9
you. Yeah.
you. Here and now,

D/C
D/F♯
G
G/B
I promise to love faith-ful-ly.
Cmaj9
F♯m7♭5
4fr
A/B
Cmaj9
You're all I need.
Here and now, I
D/C
D/F♯
G
G/B
Cmaj9
To Coda
vow to be one with thee.
1
C/D
G
G/B
C
C/D
Your love is all I need.
Stay.

G(add9)
G/B
C
C/D
2
C
C/D
When Your love is all I
Cmaj9
D/C
D
need. Start-ing here, ooh, and I'm start - ing now. I be-lieve.
G
Cmaj9
Start - ing here, I'm start - ing right here. Start - ing now,
(I be - lieve.)
C/D
right now, be-cause I be - lieve in your love, so I'm

F/G
G/B
Cmaj9
D.S. al Coda
glad to take the vow. Here and now, oh, I
CODA
C
C/D
G(add9)
Your love is all I, I, yeah,
need. Vocal ad lib.
G(add9)/B
Cmaj9
1, 2
B♭maj9
Fmaj9
yeah. Uh, yeah. Ay ah, love is all I
last time: rit.
3
C(add9)
Yeah.

MORE THAN WORDS

Words and Music by NUNO BETTENCOURT
and GARY CHERONE

* Recorded a half step lower.

Am7
C
D
Dsus
Em
want you not to say, but if you on - ly knew
have to do is close your eyes and just reach out your hands
G/B
Am7
D7
G
how eas - y it would be to show
and touch me. Hold me close, don't ev -
Bm7/F♯
Em
G/B
Am7
me how you feel. More than words is
- er let me go. More than words is
D7
G7
G7/B
C
Cm
3fr
all you have to do to make it real.
all I ev - er need - ed you to show.
Then you would-

G
Em
G/B
Em11
5fr
G/B
- n't have to say that you love me 'cause
Am7
D7
G
G/B
G
G/B
I'd al - read - y know. What would you do
D/F♯
Em
G/B
Bm7
C
if my heart was torn in two? More than words
Am
D7
G
to show you feel that your love for me is real.

G/B
G
D/F#
Em
What would you say if I took
those words a - way?
Bm7
C
Am7
Then you could - n't make things new
To Coda
D7
just by say - in' "I love you."
La di da da di da di dai dai da.
D5
5fr
More than words.

G/B
C(add2)
Am7
La di da da di da.
D7
D.S. al Coda
CODA
D7
G
G/B
C
- in' "I love you."
Am7
C
D5
5fr
D7
G
La di da da di da di dai dai da. More than words.
C(add2)
Am7
1, 2
C
La di da da di da di dai dai da.

D5
D7
G
3
C
D5
D
More than words.
More than words,
La da dat da da da.
G
D/F♯
Fmaj13
ooh,
rit.
E(add4)
Am7
D
ooh.
(Guitar cadenza)
More than
Slowly
G
Csus2
G/B
Gm/B♭
Am7
G
words.

WHEN YOU SAY YOU LOVE ME

Words by ROBIN SCOFFIELD
Music by MARK HAMMOND

B
F♯m
dream.
Like the ech - o of our souls are meet - ing,
long.
And when you touch me, if I close my eyes,
E
you say those words; my heart stops beat - ing.
I won - der what
there are times, I swear, I feel like I can fly.
For a mo - ment
3
B
D
it means.
What could it be
that
in time,
some - where be - tween
the
E/G♯
A
D6
comes o - ver me? At times I can't
move,
at times I can
heav - ens and earth, I'm fro - zen in
time,
oh, when you

D/E E6 D/E E9 A A/G♯
hard - ly breathe.
say those words.
When you say you love me, the
F♯m7 D E7 A A/G♯
world goes still, so still in - side. And when you say you love me, for a
1
F♯m7 D E7 Dsus2/F♯ E/G♯
mo - ment there's no one else a - live.
A
2
F♯m7 D E7
mo - ment there's no one else a -

A
A/G♯
F♯m7
D
E7
live.
F♯m
Dmaj7
And this jour - ney that we're on, how far we've
A
E
Fdim7
come, and I cel - e - brate ev - 'ry mo -
3
F♯m
Dmaj7
D6
ment. And when you say you love me, that's

A/E
Dm6/F
all you have to say. I'll al - ways feel this
mf
F♯m
D
E
way.
C
G/C
C
F/C
G7
When you say you love me, the world goes still, so still in - side. And
f
C
G/A
3fr
Am7
F
G7
when you say you love me, in that mo - ment I know why I'm a -

C
Fmaj7
G7
live.
C
Fmaj7
F
G
When you say you love me,
Fsus2/A
Fmaj7
Freely
C
C/B
Am7
F
G
C
when you say you love me, do you know how I love you?
mp

LOVE OF A LIFETIME

Words and Music by BILL LEVERTY
and CARL SNARE

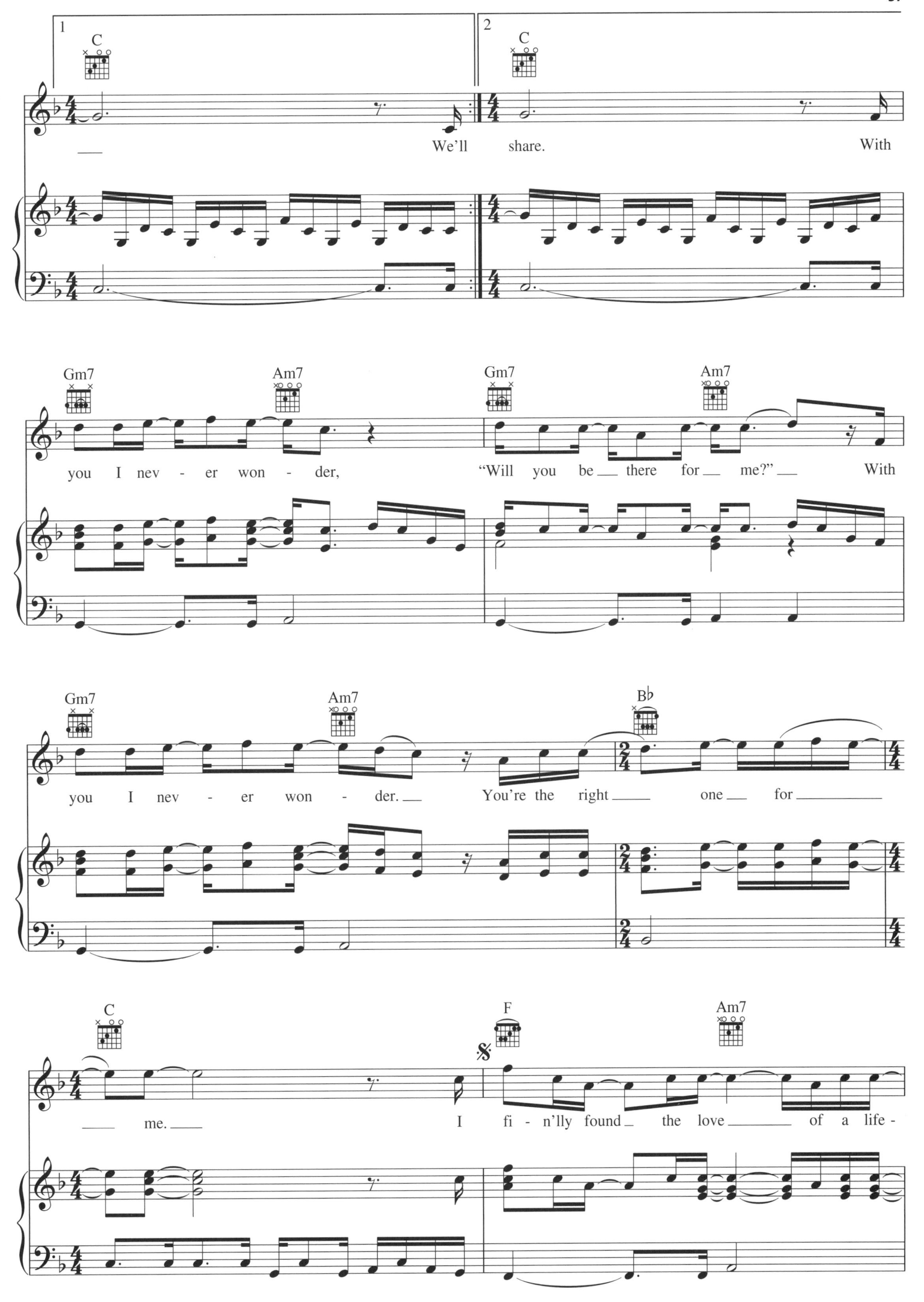
1
C
We'll
2
C
share.
With
Gm7
Am7
you I nev - er won - der,
Gm7
Am7
"Will you be there for me?"
With
Gm7
Am7
you I nev - er won - der.
Bb
You're the right one for
C
me.
F
Am7
I fi - n'lly found the love of a life -

Bb
C/E
F
Am7
- time, a love to last my whole life through.
Bb
C/E
F
Am7
I fi - n'lly found the love of a life -
Bb
C
Gm7
Am7
- time for - ev - er in my heart. I
To Coda
Bb
C
F
Am7
fi - n'lly found the love of a life - time.

B♭
C
F
C/E
With ev - 'ry kiss, our love is like brand - new
Dm
C
Gm7
Am7
and ev - 'ry star up in the sky was made
B♭
C
F
C/E
Dm
C
for me and you.
Still, we both know that the road is long,
but we
Gm7
Am7
B♭
C
D.S. al Coda
know that we will be to - geth - er be - cause our love is strong.
I

CODA
F
C/E
Dm
C
B♭
F/A
- time.
Gm7
C
Ooh
I
G
Bm7
C
D/F♯
G
Bm7
fi - n'lly found the love of a life - time,
a love to last my whole life through.
C
D/F♯
G
Bm7
C
D
I fi - n'lly found the love of a life - time for -
3

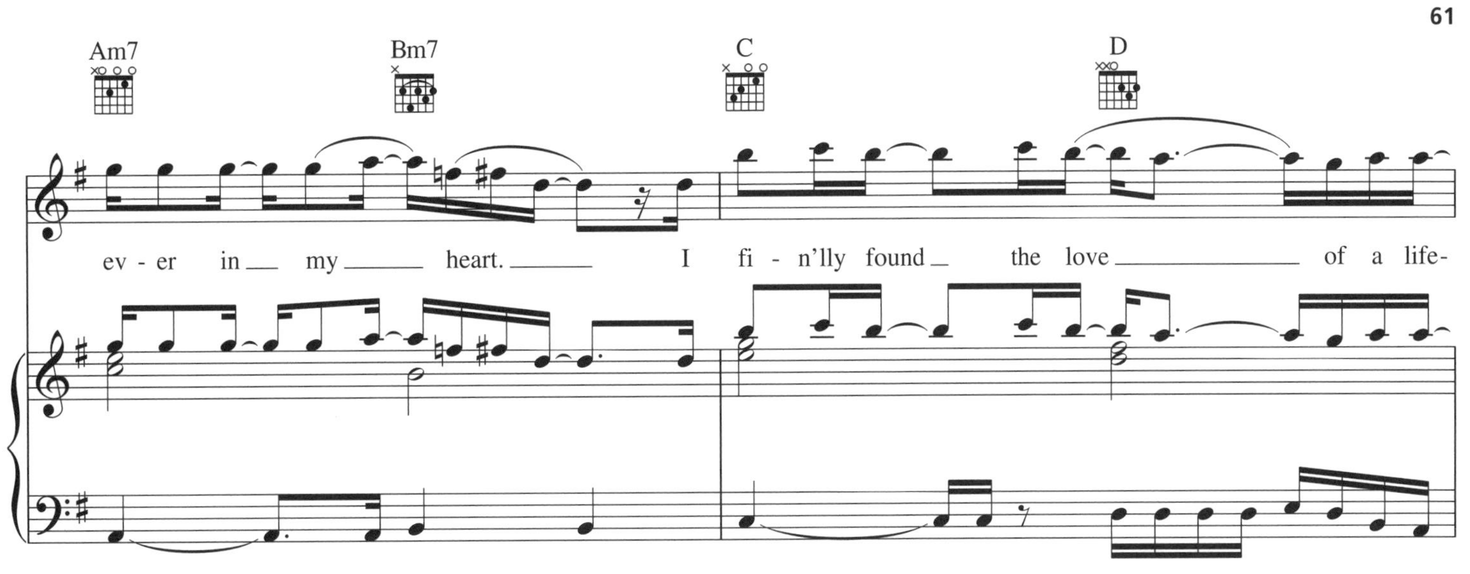
Am7
Bm7
C
D
ev - er in my heart. I fi - n'lly found the love of a life-

G
Bm7
C
D
- time, love of a life-
(Fi - n'lly found the love of a life - time.)

G
Bm7
C
D
- time. I fi - n'lly found the love.
(Fi - n'lly found the love of a life - time.)

G
Bm7
C
D
(Fi - n'lly found the love of a life - time,)
ooh, for -

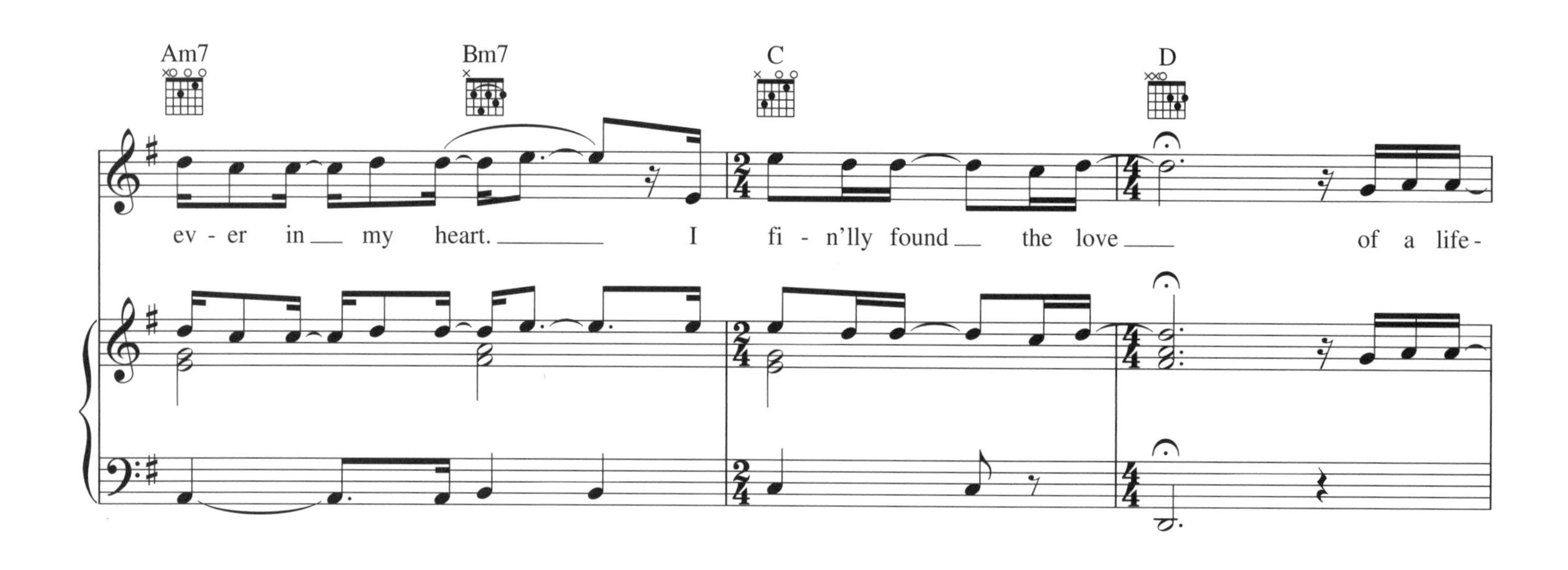
Am7
Bm7
C
D
ev - er in my heart. I fi - n'lly found the love of a life -

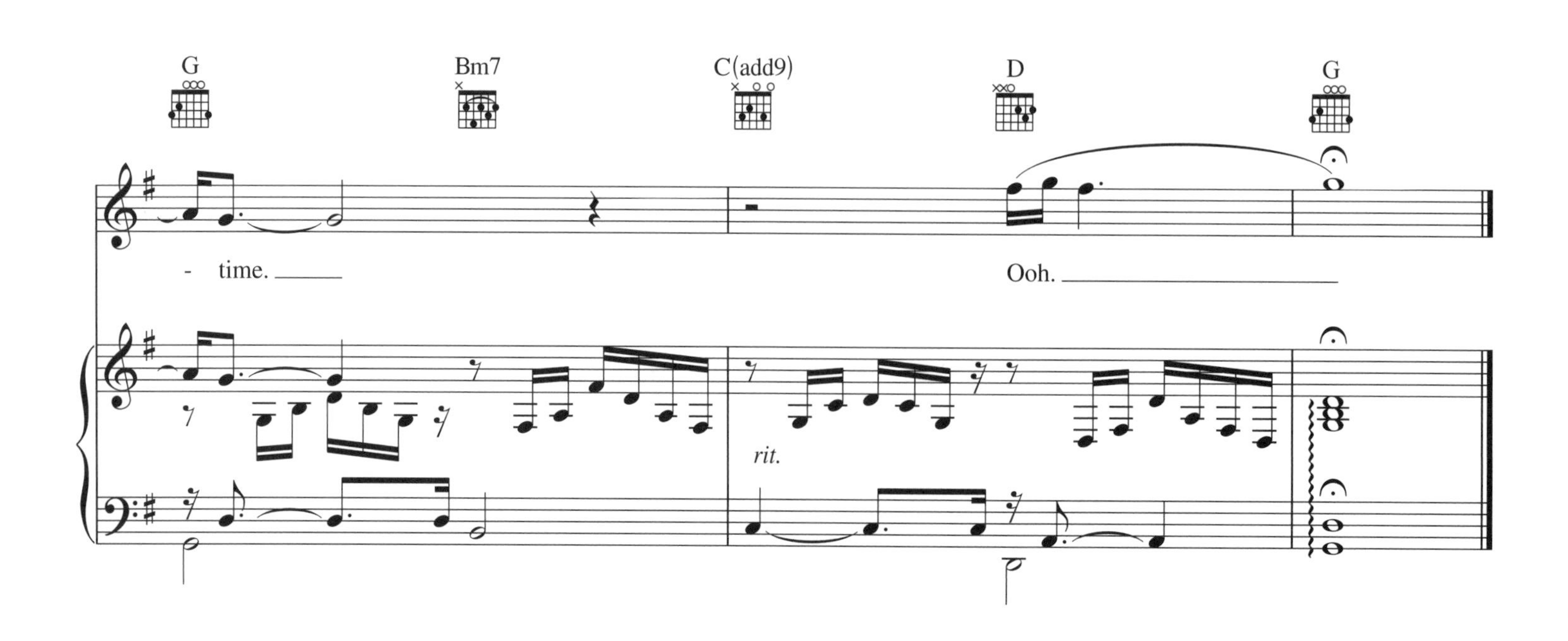
G
Bm7
C(add9)
D
G
- time.
Ooh.
rit.

The Wedding Essentials series is a great resource for wedding musicians, featuring beautiful arrangements for a variety of instruments. Each book includes a reference CD to help couples choose the perfect songs for their wedding ceremony or reception.

Christian Wedding Favorites

Answered Prayer • God Causes All Things to Grow • God Knew That I Needed You • Household of Faith • I Will Be Here • If You Could See What I See • Love Will Be Our Home • Seekers of Your Heart • This Day • 'Til the End of Time.

00311941 P/V/G.......................................$16.99

Contemporary Wedding Ballads

Beautiful in My Eyes • Bless the Broken Road • Endless Love • (Everything I Do) I Do It for You • From This Moment On • Have I Told You Lately • Here and Now • Love of a Lifetime • More Than Words • When You Say You Love Me.

00311942 P/V/G.......................................$16.99

Love Songs for Weddings

Grow Old with Me • Here, There and Everywhere • If • Longer • Part of My Heart • Valentine • We've Only Just Begun • The Wedding Song • You and I • You Raise Me Up.

00311943 Piano Solo.......................................$16.99

Service Music for Weddings

Processionals, Recessionals, Lighting of the Unity Candle

Allegro maestoso • Amazing Grace • Ave Maria • Canon in D • Jesu, Joy of Man's Desiring • Jupiter (Chorale Theme) • O Perfect Love • Ode to Joy • Rondeau • Trumpet Voluntary.

00311944 Piano Solo.......................................$14.99

Wedding Guitar Solos

All I Ask of You • Gabriel's Oboe • Grow Old with Me • Hallelujah • Here, There and Everywhere • More Than Words • Sunrise, Sunset • Wedding Song (There Is Love) • When I Fall in Love • You Raise Me Up.

00701335 Guitar Solo.......................................$16.99

Wedding Vocal Solos

Grow Old with Me • I Swear • In My Life • Longer • The Promise (I'll Never Say Goodbye) • Someone Like You • Sunrise, Sunset • Till There Was You • Time After Time • We've Only Just Begun.

00311945 High Voice.......................................$16.99
00311946 Low Voice.......................................$16.99

Worship for Weddings

Be Unto Your Name • Broken and Beautiful • Center • He Is Here • Here and Now • Holy Ground • How Beautiful • Listen to Our Hearts • Today (As for Me and My House).

00311949 P/V/G.......................................$16.99

For More Information, See Your Local Music Dealer, Or Write To:

7777 W. Bluemound Rd. P.O. Box 13819 Milwaukee, WI 53213

www.halleonard.com

Prices, content, and availability subject to change without notice.

The Most Romantic Music In The World

Arranged for piano, voice, and guitar

The Best Love Songs Ever – 2nd Edition

This revised edition includes 65 romantic favorites: Always • Beautiful in My Eyes • Can You Feel the Love Tonight • Endless Love • Have I Told You Lately • Misty • Something • Through the Years • Truly • When I Fall in Love • and more.

00359198 ....$19.95

The Big Book of Love Songs – 2nd Edition

80 romantic hits in many musical styles: Always on My Mind • Cherish • Fields of Gold • I Honestly Love You • I'll Be There • Isn't It Romantic? • Lady • My Heart Will Go On • Save the Best for Last • Truly • Wonderful Tonight • and more.

00310784 ....$19.95

The Christian Wedding Songbook

37 songs of love and commitment, including: Bonded Together • Cherish the Treasure • Flesh of My Flesh • Go There with You • Household of Faith • How Beautiful • I Will Be Here • Love Will Be Our Home • Make Us One • Parent's Prayer • This Is the Day • This Very Day • and more.

00310681 ....$16.95

The Bride's Guide to Wedding Music

This great guide is a complete resource for planning wedding music. It includes a thorough article on choosing music for a wedding ceremony, and 65 songs in many different styles to satisfy lots of different tastes. The songs are grouped by categories, including preludes, processionals, recessionals, traditional sacred songs, popular songs, country songs, contemporary Christian songs, Broadway numbers, and new age piano music.

00310615 ....$19.95

Broadway Love Songs

50 romantic favorites from shows such as *Phantom of the Opera, Guys and Dolls, Oklahoma!, South Pacific, Fiddler on the Roof* and more. Songs include: All I Ask of You • Bewitched • I've Grown Accustomed to Her Face • Love Changes Everything • So in Love • Sunrise, Sunset • Unexpected Song • We Kiss in a Shadow • and more.

00311558 ....$15.95

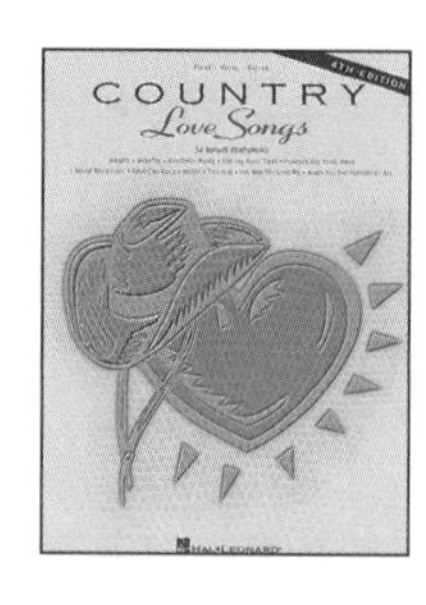

Country Love Songs – 4th Edition

This edition features 34 romantic country favorites: Amazed • Breathe • Could I Have This Dance • Forever and Ever, Amen • I Need You • The Keeper of the Stars • Love Can Build a Bridge • One Boy, One Girl • Stand by Me • This Kiss • Through the Years • Valentine • You Needed Me • more.

00311528 ....$14.95

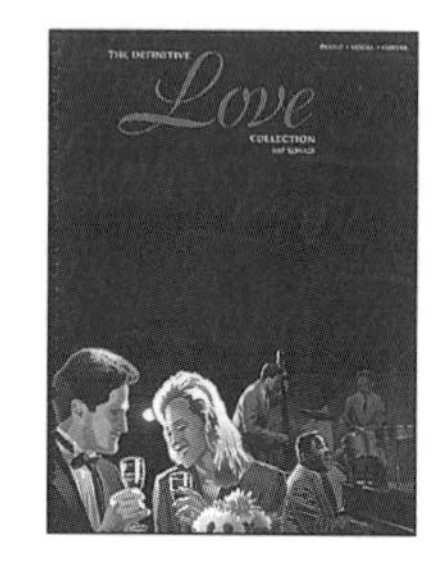

The Definitive Love Collection – 2nd Edition

100 romantic favorites – all in one convenient collection! Includes: All I Ask of You • Can't Help Falling in Love • Endless Love • The Glory of Love • Have I Told You Lately • Heart and Soul • Lady in Red • Love Me Tender • My Romance • So in Love • Somewhere Out There • Unforgettable • Up Where We Belong • When I Fall in Love • and more!

00311681 ....$24.95

I Will Be Here

Over two dozen romantic selections from top contemporary Christian artists such as Susan Ashton, Avalon, Steven Curtis Chapman, Twila Paris, Sonicflood, and others. Songs include: Answered Prayer • Beautiful in My Eyes • Celebrate You • For Always • Give Me Forever (I Do) • Go There with You • How Beautiful • Love Will Be Our Home • and more.

00306472 ....$17.95

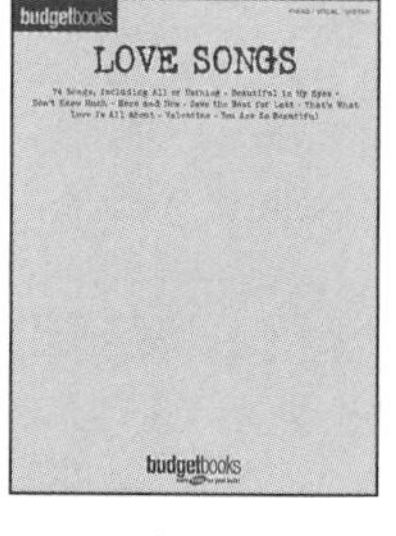

Love Songs

Budget Books Series

74 favorite love songs, including: And I Love Her • Cherish • Crazy • Endless Love • Fields of Gold • I Just Called to Say I Love You • I'll Be There • (You Make Me Feel Like) A Natural Woman • Wonderful Tonight • You Are So Beautiful • and more.

00310834 ....$12.95

The New Complete Wedding Songbook

41 of the most requested and beloved songs for romance and weddings: Anniversary Song • Ave Maria • Canon in D (Pachelbel) • Could I Have This Dance • Endless Love • I Love You Truly • Just the Way You Are • The Lord's Prayer • Through the Years • You Needed Me • Your Song • and more.

00309326 ....$12.95

New Ultimate Love and Wedding Songbook

This whopping songbook features 90 songs of devotion, including: The Anniversary Waltz • Can't Smile Without You • Could I Have This Dance • Endless Love • For All We Know • Forever and Ever, Amen • The Hawaiian Wedding Song • Here, There and Everywhere • I Only Have Eyes for You • Just the Way You Are • Longer • The Lord's Prayer • Love Me Tender • Misty • Somewhere • Sunrise, Sunset • Through the Years • Trumpet Voluntary • Your Song • and more.

00361445 ....$19.95

Romance – Boleros Favoritos

Features 48 Spanish and Latin American favorites: Aquellos Ojos Verdes • Bésame Mucho • El Reloj • Frenes • Inolvidable • La Vida Es Un Sueño • Perfidia • Siempre En Mi Corazón • Solamente Una Vez • more.

00310383 ....$16.95

Soulful Love Songs

Features 35 favorite romantic ballads, including: All My Life • Baby, Come to Me • Being with You • Endless Love • Hero • I Just Called to Say I Love You • I'll Make Love to You • I'm Still in Love with You • Killing Me Softly with His Song • My Cherie Amour • My Eyes Adored You • Oh Girl • On the Wings of Love • Overjoyed • Tonight, I Celebrate My Love • Vision of Love • You Are the Sunshine of My Life • You've Made Me So Very Happy • and more.

00310922 ....$14.95

Selections from

VH1's 100 Greatest Love Songs

Nearly 100 love songs chosen for their emotion. Includes: Always on My Mind • Baby, I Love Your Way • Careless Whisper • Endless Love • How Deep Is Your Love • I Got You Babe • If You Leave Me Now • Love Me Tender • My Heart Will Go On • Unchained Melody • You're Still the One • and dozens more!

00306506 ....$27.95

FOR MORE INFORMATION, SEE YOUR LOCAL MUSIC DEALER, OR WRITE TO:

7777 W. BLUEMOUND RD. P.O. BOX 13819 MILWAUKEE, WI 53213

www.halleonard.com

Prices, contents, and availability subject to change without notice. Some products may not be available outside the U.S.A.

1004